WHO WHISPERED NEAR ME

WHO WHISPERED
NEAR ME

KILLARNEY CLARY

BLOODAXE BOOKS

ISBN: 1 85224 149 7

This edition first published 1993 by
Bloodaxe Books Ltd,
P.O. Box 1SN,
Newcastle upon Tyne NE99 1SN.

Bloodaxe Books Ltd acknowledges
the financial assistance of Northern Arts.

Published by arrangement with Farrar, Straus & Giroux, New York.
First published in 1989 in the USA by Farrar, Straus & Giroux
and in Canada by HarperCollins.

ACKNOWLEDGEMENTS

Grateful acknowledgement is made to the following periodicals
in which some of these poems first appeared: *American Poetry Review,
Boston Review, Greenhouse Review, How(ever), Indiana Review,
Missouri Review, Paris Review*, and *Partisan Review*.

A special thanks to Gary Young, who published ten of these poems
as part of *By Me, By Any, Can and Can't Be Done*, #8 in
the *Greenhouse Review* Chapbook Series.

The front cover shows *Large Double Eye* by Mike and Doug Starn:
1990, toned ortho film, plexiglass, glue, silicone and pipe clamps,
123" x 87" x 18", courtesy of the Fred Hoffman Gallery,
Santa Monica, California, and Stux Gallery, New York, New York.

Cover printing by J. Thomson Colour Printers Ltd, Glasgow.

Printed in Great Britain by
Cromwell Press Ltd, Broughton Gifford, Melksham, Wiltshire.

For Kathleen

Contents

✍

✍

✍

When you first meet him, he may seem to be very different from you. He is not. He may seem to be very much like you. He is not.

—SALIK

We are waves whose stillness is non-being.
We are alive because of this, that we have no rest.

—ABU-TALIB KALIM

Be not therefore anxious for the morrow: for the morrow will be anxious for itself. Sufficient unto the day is the evil thereof.

—MATTHEW 6:34

As you struggle with the boat, it drifts out and turns until I see only your back, and you grow smaller, lighter, bluer on the changing of Lake Havasu—a name I think I've heard often.

Next you are in the snow; your skin is the color of roughed metal. Someone tells you to throw something or to run, to hold a useless fish as high as you can. You point to your left, not knowing that years later you will be pointing in my room. You describe something and your hands outline the shape of the screen.

I don't try to imagine that I hear you or that you had anything to do with what I see, or with your life, bounded for me by the films—a bleached Yucca Valley and a few other weekends.

The close of the reel is Christmas 1956. You lift me onto a tricycle and hold my feet to the pedals. I want to play with your teeth but you hand me more things—a book someone else will read to me, a horn that makes us both laugh.

Sacrificed so that I could be uncertain, the dead were not me. It was the end of the suburbs, Vietnam. Sprinklers on the lawn, sunlight in large rooms with wooden floors, the anxiety of having things "just so"—that sweet package was finally opened. But my dreams will not punish me enough, nor can I blame Calley, who thought if he could kill them all, he could go home. I think it's good to want to go home.

The scare leaks now into little, patient countries where the U.S. chases ghosts, where heroes fight and heroes refuse. I can't imagine the pain; I cannot feel the United States of America. I know I lost the war, but to what does knowledge bring me? An open field with no trail and cries for help from all directions? If bad is only sickness and the wrong are just misunderstood, it was a war to sap the Big Fear and there will be no answer. Like being awake all the time.

Easy as an arm moving over water, a slight wind on the bay. The seaweed roots are as locked as these heat clouds. In toured houses, amid the famous names I found names of their second cousins, paintings of a friend by another friend, a glass-cased prize fish, decomposed. Every summer I've gathered the same kinds of pieces—a broken necklace, game of cards, a chicken pockmark from a week in my mother's cooler room. I've been where my parents met so many times I am surprised to hear they were there before me. Easy as an accident, a perfect day.

Out and back—a mountain shape compacting in the distance, the name of a dead dog in a city behind the mountain. There now. Here then. There are fewer new stories every year and the old ones get smaller and quieter like a friend who waits to see if my car starts, if I make the first turn all right. An arm is drawn smoothly above the warm shallows and a tossed shell skips across, then rocks in heavy water. In the city an oak leaf is set on a gutter stream as a ticket for different weather.

Green beetles tick against the lighted window. The crickets stay. I'm irritable on the phone, feel I'm supposed to entertain you, but I've had a stupid day and my only thought is full of complaint. You're tired, and the delay on the long-distance line causes us to interrupt each other and to say with a harsh edge, "I can't hear you; I'm sorry."

It isn't worth hearing. I'm talking because if I didn't something would be wrong. "Lock up." "Get some sleep." "Where will you be tomorrow?" "There's a jet going over. Wait."

We mean it when we say "Be careful," and yet it seems now we aren't meant to talk. Talk is the pool-sweep and renewal notice, or else just a reminder that we're on the phone. What we tell about ourselves and friends snarls and tightens into a patient, black seed. No one bit reaches us both at once, and when we try to share what we've found separately, the unbodied meanings mumble and poke.

Trouble is camouflaged and of a prehistoric shape, angular, armored, and full of endurance. Each tear is streamlined. The method is passed on in a gesture: this is how to be treated and this is how to treat. If the culprit has a voice, it dipped or soared out of our range before we were born. There's no place to stop. Let's get on with it.

Because the ones I work for do not love me, because I have said too much and I haven't been sure of what is right and I've hated the people I've trusted, because I work in an office and we are lost and when I come home I say their lives are theirs and they don't know what they apologize for and none of it mended, because I let them beat me and I remember something of mine which not everyone has, and because I lie to keep my self and my hands my voice on the phone what I swallow what hurts me, because I hurt them—

I give them the hours I spend away from them and carry them, even in my sleep, at least as the nag of a misplaced shoe, for years after I have quit and gone on to another job where I hesitate in telling and I remember and I resent having had to spend more time with them than with the ones I love.

.

Every time I step into the bathtub, Theresa, I think of you; I think of your foot that was burned when you lived in Michigan. And Claire is on bridges like the Colorado where her mother fell or jumped. I think of Kathy when I see sprinklers turning in roses or I hear the name of her brother, George. Sydne in dime stores. Helen in lavender. Anne Marie with folded notes. Every time I am hit, Jeffrey, I can help, Taka. I cross the border, Billy. When I sleep, large, recent faces repeat what they've told me in the past few days, then you come toward me with names I haven't said aloud in years, each one of you faint but completed, carrying small stories—where you were once, what it was that happened. And you say, "Here." You see what I have, what you might need to tell someone else.

It's what I'm afraid of that hints at what I desire. Not this comfortable screened porch on an eastern beach in Indian summer, but holding a gun or asking favors, saying without doubt, "I wish . . ."

When I pray now, it's with puzzles of contingencies and a net of addenda. I finish in a corner, my heart bound and struggling, begging, "If it is your will, Lord, then what's the problem?" And when I don't pray, I whine, "Why should I send a letter to my friend who won't answer?"

The shore is long and nearly flat. The tendency of the tide doesn't falter; the ocean doesn't miss and doesn't adapt for me or the birds, for trash cast off a weekend cruiser. I am in the place of my dreams, still uneasy. My good anger, my best yearning, won't work toward a finish when there is none.

Clouds of birds rise above the upper bay, slant into the white sky then bank, black and full; of bees in the ashes in the pause of traffic in the lull of afternoon; of fish, silver, solid then gone, masters of camouflage by light. Swells of kelp, of cloud, of leaves in the new wind from Palm Springs, of ochre dust on the dry edge of idleness. The stores are open and the sun angles harshly onto the window displays, insulting coats on sale before inventory. Even the moon is skittish, up early and pale but whole as the sun. Old, and of a plan.

The upper bay, the glitter of it, the heavy pelican that soars only inches from the surface are an hour away through Riverside and Garden Grove. The dust is carried there in a thick haze that gathers itself between Balboa and Catalina and packs down and hovers and drones on. It's trapped and embarrassed and won't stop excusing itself with all the elements of bad luck, except to claim with pride it stands undressed.

Out there in the calm, exposed, I might look back toward home. Everything, everyone is out of place, moving or turning again, able to see both sides of any argument. And I am there. On shore, a woman sweeps her toddler off to the parking lot for reasons weak and distant to me; but I understand—some discomfort or foreboding, fatigue from blowing sand or the glare, maybe tired joy. I drift away from the determined ones on solid ground. And I am here.

An hour away. I've lived within a two-hour drive all my life. The Santa Anas cease as abruptly as they blew in; the air deadens. After it rains in these mountains, I figure the silt will cloud the channel and fan out where it, too, can remember as it leaves the peninsula and Corona del Mar. Nothing will dissolve, not boredom or urgency. The weather and moves we might have made nag like a child, "Watch me. Watch me. Look at me," before another ordinary, spectacular dive into the country-club pool.

I ride a carousel among the squid. A choir seems at the center of the turning. Their voices should be secret, furred in their bubbles, but they are marble-hard and bright as a flashing school of fish; now thinner, quieter through the church light, kelp light, they are pulled away in their hymn.

I can go back farther than any star or reason, farther back to where the song began, but my horse pulls toward the inside and I see in the axis there are no singing children.

What have I imagined in the sad water? Never quite silence or loss, never staying behind. The harmony returns and hangs in a cave, almost steady as I lead my circle in the nearly breathless, nearly finished, where I live.

The wind stopped for a moment at the end of autumn and twilight; a woman called across the yards to her young son, toward the blueing trees, tired faces of workers who glimpsed the moon beginning. Some things are only bright in the darkness. Some people never have their time. They feel like certain birds and fish designed especially to go through.

I will empty the Sunday afternoon out through a window, and part of that summer day will be what wavers in and out of light: the hiss of glittered surface that pulses across the bay, nervous boat flags. With the idleness of the lanky, a friend will chase the tall head of a friend's shadow as it dips and wags on the pavement and for a few minutes everything will seem empty. Those still on the beach that late will sigh and resettle into positions closer to sleep.

Stalled on this hazy spring Friday, I try building myself for that long season because once inside it I will forget so much. Even the stagnancy of my face in an unchanging face of air I will forget, though it will all be in an adjusting sigh, in the yearning for a touch, a little warmer, a little cooler, on the shocked skin and brittle time, a little less light or more.

I ask for none of this now. I am tired of the differences that add up to what comes in or goes out and the measure of how far, tired of the continual arrangements I make with my clothes and the weather to keep myself appropriate, a fair balance for the variable. But I am uneasy with the slips of August into this day. I am here too early in the year and I am afraid of something on the waterfront—sounds that are fainter because they have every way out, the man who comes in long pants and long-sleeved shirt to see something so large and uninterrupted as this ocean. He sits in the fog and I am afraid of his black shoes that sit next to him and shine.

Life is boundless. Matter is without edge. We grow always outward from ancient explosions and the heavenly bodies distance themselves from each other, then steady, balanced with various pulls. There is a new place.

Like a cartoon, like a promise that we, too, could buy new cars and eat anything, Armstrong bounced his puffy life onto the powder of the moon. We were all watching, tired of the delays.

If there is too much to keep track of, or if it is simply discouraging or overwhelming to live in the world, there is a hideout which can look something like the Sea of Tranquillity. There is aimlessness like dust in a light shaft. There are alternatives now: vacant expanses, time's measure lost, the emptiness that turns us inside and prods us empty and stupid like that funny flag he kept trying to straighten—taffeta-stiff and unruly. And then it stood out flat.

Disappointed in the dead moon, we could believe the myth of abandon, the giant step of surrender. We tired young, each begging, "Take me, weightlessness, where it is quiet, dark-sky'd and clean."

Near four o'clock the daylight changes into a way of leaving. Spring, and across the city heat rises into attics, lingers, and grows tired. I tell myself not to go home in the afternoon and I think hard about a leaf on the concrete, the sound of tires rubbing the curb. Children in cars. Anne is waiting up the sidewalk for a station wagon. Under the trees. The game is just a sound for us, of a bat and ball above the field out on Waldo Avenue. Anne is so quiet I don't need to watch for her ride. She seems all right as she moves her eyes along the row of wooden houses, up the guy wire for the telephone pole, down to a sore at her thumbnail.

I know you, Anne, through high school, past this part of the city into another. We grow up this sadly along with the spray-painted "Ogre" and "Stinky Felix" that watch from the La Loma and even taller bridges, names placed for danger. With their quick power, they are certain they won't be covered.

Anne waits with the gradual shade. Her life is more confused than mine, so she carries her place in her clean skin. I tell myself not to go home in the afternoon when the air has no time or smell, to a place where I can imagine the interruptions are unvaried, dependable. It is so close to being true. Anne won't call goodbye as I leave; she'll become the afternoon, with a face that moves little.

I will go home with my mother; on the way we drive past other things I know. They are so close to being with me whenever I want. If I can make myself sad, I can be sure. So when my mother apologizes for being late, I don't an-

swer her but think of Anne sitting on the low wall on Belle-
vue Drive. She is still there, and my mother is sad and I am
sad and we are almost home.

Of all the signs in the world, I wonder which carries a message between us now, and what is it I am determined to tell you? You shouldn't have died, shouldn't be that permanent illusion up with the full moon behind a few hot clouds in the long night when I try to remember how you were. I should have known more than a fleck of blood on your tooth, the blue and yellow you liked best, or should have abandoned what I couldn't know, what might have worked had I the nerve to try you, had I spoken or given you a key.

So I must surrender the power to know and to grieve. It isn't my place. I want to believe you are just dead like anyone I lied to, then never saw again. Dead like someone to whom I will tell how I feel, later. You've been a ghost to me so long; it is now you take on substance. And I mourn the idea of tomorrow, a chance to see and be seen under other circumstances.

Boys on street corners in Santa Ana are selling flowers, a suggestion, different for each car. You are on your way, take something. And it is on into the night like this that people go. They call from phone booths in gas stations. They hear their shoes in the cold.

Behind the restaurants, a searchlight reaches up and over.

I have spent warmer nights closer to the coast, listening to older children laughing bravely in the dark bay. The night water must have been all they could feel until a siren whined down the peninsula and they wanted to be sure of what touched them. Plumbing. Wiring. Big-eyed rodents. The people are waking up in China.

A boy picks up his plastic bucket in one hand. Parked-car radio. Restless horse.

It can't be like night to die, with the world right here— even the moon and cut of clouds, even the gradual shower on the asphalt, on the apartment roof, when down the row windows are closed against the water and someone tells someone else, who already knows, it is raining. I am not likely to sleep or die out of this.

Chinamen drink their tea. They wear loose clothes like these sheets. Into this night they are rising.

Someone starts a car below my window and pulls out under the storm. I want to know where they are going. The man in back who sells firewood is out to check his yard—a cow, ducks, one goose standing guard at the parking-lot fence.

The boys are at home in Santa Ana; their flowers are passengers in dark cars. Someone drives them and the lights go by.

Don't tell me you give up here like it's a puzzle you think someone else has solved so why not ask them; the ones with that answer are quiet.

Take light. Goodbye. Silvered skin in deep water. I am afraid of "Where are you?" For sound, I would take a voice from the next room turning into sleep. But where? Take heart; take shelter. There, there now.

The girls in the office are afraid of Lynn's ghost. She'd been there, alive, working at her desk last week. I was only angry. A cough like a dog that won't be shut out. Her body, finally. Be a ghost at least, Lynn, not so far away—heaven or nowhere—not so different.

It was in November when the nights were cold with certainty in a dim town covered with stars and leaves. Dark wind closed the eyes of a crier who rang his bell, calling, "Wake, you sleepers; the dead cannot weep." The ones who heard him beg to come on now with the sirens, fall down in the rain.

Comfort of vapor, soothe goodbye. I will, as they must, miss the world so.

I set out a cardboard box of seed for the sparrows and finches, propped it on a forked branch of the olive tree in the courtyard. In the late afternoon the small birds gathered; a fat dove settled into the box with them. I went inside, my bare arms cold, and in the kitchen I wondered at the dark yard. I didn't know it had grown so late—the windows, black; the safe world, closing.

Past the bold, fast jays and fruit trees, the syrup hung in jars for hummingbirds, and olives on the brick—I go from the house of china doll on the top shelf, of pencil cup in its place.

Jay-thief in the parsley, I leave you the garden—hearts of carrots, radishes, beets—because they'd grow in their plot in their strong, rock way. You want my good-nights in baskets, whatever you'll fight the window for—marbles and scarves, blackberries in a dish or stained on lips, the magic slippers—because, you say, it's a small garden, really.

Through the water, deeper than the seeds of chives or tomato, out of the silk and cat's eye, out of the voice of story, the catch is huge. Up through the ocean the bright grains angle toward me into the lens that gathers all light to one spark.

As the roofing breaks up, you perch on a rotted shingle, jerk your black eyes, tilt your head, check, watch, jump down. You find the touch of dust, tired colors of a lampshade and a song to make you bow. I told you I didn't want to leave the walls I was born with. The air has always let me through.

My ship moves off in the night for spices and easier routes at a height to which I am not yet accustomed. If it catches in a raft of kelp I will picture you uprooting and if the damp air thickens I will call for charts to make up for the weakened light.

Sharp jay. Sharp rocks on the jetties, black shoulders for the harbor. Take time on the outlines. Sharp bird, wearing down, the air grows softer for you. Unsteady on the bed-post and unsure of your eyes, you ask, where was that shining bend, the edges of glass on a dresser top, patterned paper. They are dull now as the darkness begins to repair the roof, as the black ocean moves from me with its great tale of making way.

Have we proved our wealth or kindness? There is slight difference. I listen to a friend who tells me her problem. What is her need, so easily met by my company, hidden from me after we say good night? What do I do now?

I remember. The hands that turned the almost-empty glass for hours. I remember certain lonely places on the street where I had to stop for a signal or a train. It's easy to do what I set out to do, but so what? Even what people misunderstand of each other sinks down and waters a wholly different future. I wanted everyone to say I was good. She wanted to be understanding. It's such a tiny life, I can hardly see it anymore. Smaller than the stars and reckless as memory. It is such an odd desire—to be this or that.

I remember wanting to leave the empty playground because it would be raining soon—anyone could tell—and the metal rings on their heavy chains and the worn swings swayed slightly as if the others had left only minutes before. I knew better; I'd been paying attention. The world is mine. I take it up or leave it as I excuse myself or bide my sadness over some little thing—the warmth inside my ears and mouth, the chill of coming and going.

Larger than hand-passed dangers await us. Clouds and cancers. We don't work them through to Science or God and reconcile ourselves to them. We are angry at death, cheated.

Raised to a New World View—that all things wear down to one and the same—we heard the aberrations were most extreme. The neighbor boy was "not at all well." Then, as we recognized intolerance, we thought carefully about murder and considered the poor man who lived on. Our reactions slowed. We feel guilty.

Accidents. Connections. Not fate or justice but chance. So we don't pray, or hope, or work methodically toward an end. We live proudly, busily—coping always with how to free-up time. We are sincere and self-conscious, like nervous laughter.

But it was lovely in the dark hall as we shuffled and settled, close and murmuring as the sky supposedly fell in. My elbows to the wall, my hands at the back of my neck, I wondered who whispered near me, who because of circumstance might have touched me that day—Mary Ellen or Phillip. It was the last Friday of the month as the siren held its note and across the city people checked their watches. Yes, I would eat my cheese sandwich later and would even find my sweater.

Now we are confused, send condolences to TV characters who have been sickened for the sake of our need to spend time. Gather and spill. We are afraid we will know too soon the year, perhaps the month when we will leave. We want the world to last and each of us to die separately. But then, in a way, we were all born together.

I want a solution. So, "God," I pray, "finish this one un-wavering note, at any cost, song or silence." I'm afraid I don't care; afraid someone might find out even in my sore the wrinkle continues, the same future. God's familiar with my tricks—precise requests, then total surrender—, familiar with tomorrow too, and my billion dreams. He will forgive me them, but forgiveness is an added step.

I want to see the air itself dissolve, the colored powders which are you or me scatter and fade, and no, I don't care for another try. It is kindness that puts the world in my hands for me to hate; fortune that opens the surface which is, after all, beauty.

I'm sure there are endless reasons and answers, methods by which I might change. Give them to someone who de-serves them, along with my good luck and what "science" can put to use.

My whispered song, the tune replaced by breath, weakens, loses its place in a thin, icy draft. The cold lowers, by the rules. What turns a whisper to full sound pulls the colors from gray. Shaky, it skips like a stylus until time hints there is hope. But there is no more logic in this power to persevere than there is to the placement of Los Angeles or the ease on the faces of men and women who finish their long ride in. What clicks on or off after months of indecision? Did I choose to give in?

As I drive deeper into the corridor of downtown where the wind is crooked and fast between the office towers, as I try again the brightest song, I know the dead sailor who changed his mind in last night's dream will stay with me for days; I won't be afraid. And yet the friend who says good night on the phone is gone. I own nothing; I don't know my spirit. In sleep where the counting can't survive, I hear songs I've never heard, though there are no premonitions, only the teases of anxiety and fantasy. If I could turn my eyes from the experiment, it would run on smoothly with pure, unstudied results. Instead, I send off questionnaires, and wait.

Water dripped from a gray wedge; tapped for the sawdust thrown on oil, for the rat under the workbench who dreamt of white ankles and whose heart drummed in the good lumber; tapped back for me the names of tools, how I'd handed them away as they were called. Spider on a plane, bubble in the level—braced—and it was quiet in the cupboards of soup and condensed milk, in rolled maps of the China Sea, and in my favored red vise. Except for the water, yes.

It was a measure, amid the smell of cold metal, its intervals crowded with: in-progress, cleanup, and blood under a thumbnail. As in a dark church, articles gathered on three sides, in alcoves and chill. To the garden-wall bricks I'd chipped with a hammer, to the convex streets, their gutters receiving, the space was jammed with division.

The yard back-fenced on another yard where a boy played privately with the rain. Beyond, there were miles of heaviness, the last minutes of work, and then it was nearly dinnertime; people pulled their bright, steaming cars into garages. I moved quickly with the earth and the atmosphere that held to it, but I could still reach a jar of nails and walk away with the steadiness of a good spin.

I believe in time as healer and destroyer, wind that will not rest, and I believe in stars and tides yet all I see is delayed. I imagine I was born though it feels like surrender and I know I will die but won't leave anyone.

I was appointed certain tasks and goals when I reached certain ages. How easy it is for me to tie a shoelace and drive a car. Who tells me now?

I believe in promises—that we are obligated by a simple word that couldn't be held back. I will be there if you need me, if you can reach me, if I can hear you.

I thought I should be alone until loneliness had no meaning, but knowing if I am right is an ugly luxury. May my heart be louder in the endless test I overlook for a sure sign. I fear my last excuse will be that I didn't know what to do.

I'm sorry I brought it up. I'm sorry until I lose my body. I shouldn't have said what I said, not yet or not so late.

I answer, "I love you, too," and think, "for as long as you will believe it." But what I don't say now only thins the travel in and out of my heart, traps me in channels between my one thought and my next. So the one promises I will be new; the other laughs through its nose and says, "Sure."

If I'm daring you to please me, I have to stop somehow, but when I see what I've done wrong I am still wandering disagreeably, doing the wrong thing.

I hope I don't like you, myself, or anyone else. I hope I don't like the next song. If I do, I'll only try to remember it, and I'll have to look forward to hearing it again.

I may love this difficulty. The stars, harsh in this dry night, are points of concentration. The few notes of music that come into me surely—I draw their aim. I am feeling what I am in and I am not alone. If I believe in solution, I may consider this attention to what is here a way of moving. Still, with each supposed mark of time comes definition. Things, people, my own heart break into parts that begin to see each other and newer, tighter boundaries for themselves, and clarity as I go further in, farther away from my fingers on the lip of a bowl. My skin is one thing, my veins another, my blood. My skin is built in layers beginning to resist each other. Now. Now I am not alone with myself. If I don't know I can turn around to collections—the voice of a friend, the meeting of what I want with my forever wanting—then remind me of confusion, the sky, the whole song, beyond them, beyond what I carry out from my life, and rest. Tell me about ease, how it can soften the brightest points as if it were working. Dangerous and necessary, it is daytime. I say hello. I accomplish. I will tell you that I need, from an open, strong place, and that I may long for the possibility of losing. The certainty is over for now I am here afraid I may need to feel afraid in order to feel I know you are here. Here. Now. I know. I will act upon you.

With everything. What I am doing, not what I imagine doing. A good chance, my friend. Some kind of life should feel right, a good chance. The reasons undress themselves until they are stupid—reasons for caring about one person or another. No one is left behind; that makes the pull of each tie stronger. My fingertips swell and darken; my feet grow heavier. Whatever I have moves out to my edges until I feel nothing inside and the emptiness calms me, calms me against possibility. There is no more sheltered place than this calm; nothing can turn or break in the slow and pretty way the light carries what I see. Before I am paler, before the real draining begins, I must learn to feel without explanations, let the reasons fall to shame, and to understand. What anyone I care about is really doing. From the cold place that becomes "I'm winning" I will come up in front of them. Clear, clear as a pause, as a dream so thorough it is forgotten. Clearly, I cannot fail.

I may take the difficulty, turn it into the life that feels right, and stretch it out until I am stretching beyond my body, my words, beyond what I can think or sense as deeply as I can sense, farther beyond all that. I may love it all being that far away. Out into everyone else—everything—so I may have no fault. Still, I can't tear myself apart and wanting will be my fault endlessly. I try to step back, inhale and act amid the care. Consider waiting. Consider it forever. Start over. With nothing. What I'm not doing. With the decisions that emerge from the worry of those who love me and the way things happen. If I let what happens scatter me, remind me I am trying. I may be mistaken. The music unfolds but remains a secret. Like all secrets, it is a very small door that could open on entirety. I may be mistaken for one who balances what I absorb with what I offer. There may be no mistake. If I am confused, tell me about certainty, the dependable way in which we continue, breath and planets, back and forth on a good day, unsteady impasse of best obstacles through which I whisper, "If only . . ." And what if we are to believe in solutions, in what we've found on our way here. The problems keep us talking; what won't we do to keep talking? If only

I knew I wanted the good, if only the stars held their distances, the progressions were revealing, the doubts were bearable or plain enough to be beaten. Assure me. Trouble is a present thing; I am listening to you. You mustn't lie. Assure me.

Confidant, do we place our trust here, deep in the heart of trouble? Do we allow the bit of separation that makes us talk and sway? We can depend on it. I walk into the solitude of I-am-saving-you, a walk I don't feel, a viewing of colors and shapes that walk against me. You have done the same. I will tell you everything but now, habitually, I am leaving. At the point of my departure I hesitate. Should I call you up one more time? We can rely on the outcome, the raising of spirits in our understanding, our variable guilt. "Don't worry about me," we both say. "Is there anything I can do?"

She was sick and we had gone ahead of her through the gardens and attics, resting here in a cool grotto. She couldn't have died, we reasoned, because she would have had to pass us. We had gone ahead and left her in an easy chair—her clothing unfastened, elastic braces around her stomach. Then we must have looked back through the arbor and the rooms over the garage.

I was alone when I found her. She was still my sister but happier and she looked like someone else. I believed her but knew my mother wouldn't. And I forgave her anything; she was only responsible to stay giddy and senseless. No one should worry about her again.

I lean on Sunday morning against a warm, pink, cinder-block wall until I am warm too.

Maybe because his mother is dying, F.X. believes cancer is a state of mind, or bad timing—on a particular day a certain doctor notices an abnormality.

But I am just feeling the sun, out by the laundry room, while Ralph reads the paper. Just running my thumb over a stain without much care. I see the weave, then, and how the dye has filled it. It is something I can see. Chilled blue under my nails, coin in the slot. I will stay out here all day, I think. I am in charge of this, between weather and the microscopic.

Sleep was streams of red and white lights curving through the passes. I saw them from a melancholy, silent and weary. I want to fall in love every moment. The ache is fine and selfish, so huge and sad. If someone were here tonight, he would know what I should do with my arms which are so heavy and the numbness spreading from my spine. I might talk with him and learn how to find places for the gifts. If there were skin other than my own or a certain need. Time wears the dazzle of the small lights. I am chilled. I begin to smell the trees. Sleep was all that was left. A small and comfortable boat on the whole ocean.

I hadn't been a superstitious person. But the tissue phantom drifted across the night freeway, but the rook perched on top of the door. Yesterday, when you went to New York, everything you left here was white. You carried a photograph of someone I don't know. I try not to miss you.

I know your presence would tame my nervous study of things and their arrangement. I might not notice the quickness of the clouds tonight, the matches. Your voice would settle the way one thing should follow another, would stupefy my fear, and your hold would quiet the lines of everything leading everywhere. If I didn't feel your need now I would surrender mine, for this hour at least as I push through it; I would have to surrender until I might find I'd lasted. But what I want.

What lasts of us, in millions of places, what lasts is set aside to wait: white shoes, white pants, a box of envelopes. We last in all the things we have put here and there and we never know who notices or how those things touch their discoverers. We hold on to other times as though origins could adapt. Gradually, nothing can happen here, can happen now. The layout of palm fronds on the road that evening, the palm switch on my doorstep, lights going out as I had predicted, as we slept, as we dreamed of rain while it rained.

So I smooth my hair back off my forehead and that is you and you are not. It is me. It is my wanting. You will return, different from anything that is here now. Tired, you'll take off your shirt in the dark. You'll sit down and tell me what has happened and the rest will wait. I want to be with you.

I imagine. From that I reach the severest longing, missing the sound of the world, recalling the child who brushed by me in the market, feeling what is left, wanting more. I am not sad for what I've lost, only over the absence of what I have now, what I try to have when all I can own are things and all they can do is dissolve my belief in their backgrounds. I take the past. I love it sharply. When you return we will talk to each other; the car will be waiting; our warm clothes, our ages will be waiting. On us, between and around us, in places we've forgotten, we endure.

I must resist trying to be your heart, must hear my name in the night as a meaningless arrangement of the wind and what it passes. Wind and stars, meaningless and huge, always here, always moving. I mustn't let myself evoke what isn't me, or forget other people who are, plainly, in other places, surely. Good. The world is simple. In spite of my desire, the world is simple.

What if we do need four candles to lift our spirits into another world? Sarah wanted to tell us that we were loved, that we are all always loved, but that didn't solve her uneasiness, saying goodbye to a dying friend.

It would be a comfort to the sick if they could hear our prayers, even our twisted hopes for an end, even the scared gratitude. It would be a way to let go of senses.

Yellow flame, ivory wax, yellow-skinned sleep. Sad, unholy music of long, silent July days behind the windows and out of the heat, wrapped in the promise of illness. Fire seems so much a living thing and the smoke so unclean.

Sarah, do you believe you are loved? Your heart yearns to tell us and then seems darkened and afraid. Yellow flame draws on its wick, sputters in panic then eases tall again. Believe, cease to believe. We cannot do otherwise.

Before the birds awaken, after the possum has gone home, for a moment no one is commuting from a night shift or to an early job.

Or it's late in the afternoon, all napping. Then there is no need to tell anyone.

I need to do something else when my friend is miserable and the music is over, when my balance is off.

Everyone's binging. I talk all day about escrow and interest. I drive a long way home from work and each time I start out feeling one way and arrive feeling the opposite. Resolutions are worthless in this swamp.

Before the birds, I might assemble a way. But it is logic and figuring, pushing me far to a dead end in a maze. I won't convince with trickery. I won't move or rest with it.

There seems nothing more sad. I was in love with you. We were lost, not by defense of our pasts, but by comfort and our ways. Unsteady wonder. I doubt our time. I thought I would tell you that I, too, was unsettled, but when I walked inside where only your things were, placed and uncomfortable, where you'd put one light on, an opaque shade. Dark beach air, two chairs. Cold, the closet, your jacket. When I came in I was relieved. I knew I wouldn't say. And presence caused us to feel smaller. Less chance, fewer fair things. This is my heart, my trying. I would go home from weeks of worry. I knew less. I was certain.

What we are called is specific now. What would it mean if I could touch you? Consolation, because we will be afraid for a while? We are more. Nothing ends, nothing takes us back, forgives, repairs. What I understand of you. Nothing stops.

This is what I wanted. The adaptability of things. Continents still drifting, different light sources causing multiple shadows, shadows darkening, abandoning each other in the bright morning wind. This. Awake in seeing. To call myself apart from is to lift myself into a necessary ease, ease myself away from calling for now, for the sake of recognizing this is a time. You are there and I can do something. Surrender and abide, or challenge, or remain, watching.

An ache of what was. I will miss the illusions, the cold voice coming home on schedule for each of us, habits of reason. I may miss the lack of music, lack of hearts' questions. A cold echo below our news. In. Love. The sky is starless; the oceans are glassy. All that, too, is enclosed between dark walls with which we still try protecting each other. Bordering the reaches of encumbrance, skin that is restraint only, never touched or breathed upon. Where the edges meet, it is our separate selves still trying in a room.

We help by faltering. There is an unsolvable part that holds us faltering. Caught in assumption, we were very close, balanced by a past that was made of avoidance. A silent sail on the bay at night, drifting through the lights of August homes, away from those warm shores, a lovely passage into our loss. If it all had been secret, I wouldn't think of you or wonder if I asked too much by not asking. What names we have for each other are wrong and I wander in solution, thinking, always, of what—by me, by any—can and can't be done.

After work, after meals for Raul and her mother, Mary Lou will leave for Niland because her niece is in trouble and her father won't talk. She will stay with them in Niland, clean his house and shop for food. She will try to listen without shame.

She asks me, "What's it like to be rich?" and I say, "Only my parents have money," but she waits. "I don't worry. I have nothing to prove." It seems a lie; I want so much to convince her we are alike.

Late on Friday night, Mary Lou leaves for the desert. After driving on an unnamed road, she pulls up to the dark house and waits a few minutes without the radio. Near the border, in the bright heat, she will scold the girl, call her a whore, and very late on Sunday she will come back without thanks or success. She expects none.

Why she bothers, what good it will do, she knows better than to wonder. She's proud of the secrets, each angry, careful step on a simple map.

When my heart asked for a way free, it was led into this lightless room. In the back neighbor's kitchen window a woman stands at the sink board eating eggs quickly. Eleven o'clock night cat and traffic. Bamboo leaves and wind between here and a next place. It could be lonely. Cold business suits of tired men after airplanes from San Francisco mostly. Something for them to eat, too, and fewer stars. Awful lights, corridors, ugly ceilings. Gloom, spirited in comfort hills. Dark-shoed children in a playground. A smooth-faced dull girl with her blue dress dreams on something near the fence—stained patch of sand from last night's rain. Good friends talk about thunder. A letter to the corner leisure in an almost warm afternoon passing people as if it was Sunday. Then it's all memories. I could do something for you. You wouldn't know; you would feel better and I'd stay quiet as if it were fair.

There are more of us. We came out of a time when birth was happy.

We are prizes. Perhaps we shouldn't have been so important, so healthy. If any of us suffered war, we were pained less by the enemy than by our ability to kill him.

Our number seems a useless power. We were sold on dissatisfaction—now we're sold families but they're no sign of survival this time.

I am very lucky but that's not life. And maybe no more than any person born in any year, I want but don't know what, feel unsettled in a sea of similarly restless faces. The breadth of possibility makes choosing seem evasive. We decide but we are slow and small with doubts.

It was 1954 when my parents moved to have room for me. I remember a box my mother packed for me to store at school, filled with canned milk and soup and Hershey bars.

Two thousand good nights. My checked uniform on a hook. My face to the hall light because that felt like a day in the sun. Not fear, not loneliness, but my preference for sleeping near the window and near the floor, humming.

Someone else. And the empty time, now, in all I gather and promise. I think I can stop losing by a conversation I will have. I cross my fingers to break a habit. Where did I get those lavender sachets; where is Helen now?

The light and time move through the day together; I clear them from all the things around me until the receding and the coming up are mine. They re-form as annoyances. Where did I put that? When was the last day?

Across the cold beach, Helen and I walked toward the rocks. Up to see the sunrise. It would be light for hours before we saw the sun itself come over the cliffs. But it was too early to talk about anything. Neither of us would have been there alone. Back in the city, Helen walked from her house to mine in the summer and when I opened the door she didn't seem relieved. She wouldn't drink any water. She would stay for only a few minutes. Tired and hot. Sweat and the powdery dust from the streets and dull leaves—on her pale, fat arms and legs, on her damp shift.

It wasn't Helen but the things that seemed to become bored with me. The way her skin and hair were things. So I remember all that in the worst times. When I'm surrounded and have no fear and no regard, across years of waiting I draw my rehearsed exchange. Would you undermine it, Helen, for the best for now?

There is no way to know what I miss, and yet there is
nothing else I try to do. What happens takes very little
time; it's easy play. Before, I wonder how you will be. Will
you feel like talking about Kathleen or the babies? Will you
ask me where I was when you called? And as you ask I
wonder what you're thinking while you watch a cruiser
back out of a slip and turn toward the breakwater, Catalina,
and maybe beyond.

What was it in that moment in your voice, in the pause,
which told me? I keep working on ways through, which
narrow as I wonder harder. If I am very careful, I might
know the shift in weather between us is your bit of worry
or remembrance; I excuse you forever. I will miss you less
this way when you must go.

White sand, tall grass. This strip of ocean is a thin bit of deep blue as if the earth bends suddenly out there, beneath the dark storm moving, pushing shadows on the surface of the sea which presses in close and rushes away. A cold wind feels impatient, too, as it returns in force with each break, again. And the sky that splits is a surprise, sending a straight shaft of silver to claim its town of luck. Doors blow open with a crash, close gently a ways away. They would close.

The sun is faith and will be for so many months of empty houses, linen closets, shelves of cold glasses, while the unending sand in the undying wind heckles the clapboards, blasts the paint.

Sometimes everything is all right except my ears are cold. I think, if only my ears were warm again. If only again, want. Away. A whistle in the wind. If something changed it all forever . . . It is all changing always forever. Certainly the fish must swim deeper and birds leave for a while. In the back of a school desk a scrap of paper learns its folds until they are weak, and the penciled joke is lost in the creases, graphite dust.

There is no imitating the weather, no remembering but a dullness I think is near my heart. And when I am asked to carry out the one fine thing from the burning house, I'll know what reflects me is arbitrary; I am invisible. Won't my habits be undercut while the paces across a familiar room are smoke and ash, distance no more? I don't know myself without these clothes—the buttoned coat of answers and shoes of home.

Lightning. And the mile between. Thunder. Pulse. Wink. The moon is bright and full above the desert. Moonshadows of Joshua trees, though cool, never hint of water. So water is the treasure, a kind word, late, only half understood. And the secret moves off in time like the elves' ships in the mist of the moon. And that which faintly glows whispers to "be still," so what I cannot hold might whirl about me, so I might feed upon it and listen—to the stars which assemble with regard, again, and my heart out of beat with that less constant rhythm, that funnier dance.

A man has a cabbage, a goat, and a fox which he must take across a river. But his boat will hold only one of these at a time and he can't leave the cabbage with the goat because the goat will eat the cabbage and he can't take the cabbage or the fox will eat the goat.

If either he or I could move fast enough, all figuring would be silly; as it is, the animals are nervous. But it's not that humiliating—going back to the boat launch, carrying old baggage. When the day is through, the irritation is a joke, and as I unpack the groceries, the parakeet surprises me by asking, "Want some tea?"

He dreamt of too large a ship which only he could sail. In the tropics, the shadows of the swift clouds raced across the broad deck and, over time, the colored, triangular flags on the head stay were whipped to bright shreds and he started to hum.

Or was it again the grassy rise without a tree, the perfect sky that he climbed toward without progress? He said, "This is a dream I will outsmart," as he gained the crest and looked down upon a small village, which, though miles distant, kept no secrets.

Building his house again, he knows what he did wrong. What lives on is not children or the estate but the immeasurable now through which he moves toward the country of flying squirrels and the boundless view. He puzzles while awake that if he keeps on going half the remaining distance, he will never arrive, and he smiles at his plan in mind tonight, before he is tired and the wind dies and the shops close. It's a very good plan.

You're bent in the reeds and behind you feathers alight on the lake, tremble to the shadow of a cloud. Water, brush, then hills darken. Your restless hands in the rough lawn turn grass blades into whistles. Sun again now on the colored boats, but you cannot see that brighter clutter. Ducks bobbing and knocking near the pilings. Funny, the burden of their weightlessness. A flag, sail, shirt, a ribbon of crepe paper caught on wire. Your eyes follow the sound of a crow in back of me.

In the closet of your dark body, I forget what were, for you, the icy flowers of your own need; I leave their translucence—what we cannot help. And leaving is different from something learned or comfort or afternoon, less brave than understanding how the place behind me widens and deepens in your life. How it is good as it fits me here, between.

Breathless. White lights in the trees. They call the color Dusty Rose—of napkins folded to be birds, of tablecloths, tables padded so the china presses. Pittosporum. Pale, they say. I'll be all right. I put my foot against the chair leg.

Down. Like its own place. Warm water and repetition. But there's a nearly empty plate. I can't hear because I'm thinking of what I hear. And though the evening's balmy, still, the leaves are all moving. The sky gives and I'm rising as I fall into a calm like tears with my chilled body and the little flame.

I was thinking of a different hand. Not thinking. A dress party near the lake. Paper lanterns, inconstant light, the comfort of black water and someone beneath it who hears me. I said I would like to walk at night. Now the faces are turned down or away, buried in warm limbs. The man who takes me to dance has his big, dark hand on the center of my back, but I am thinking of the grid of wire on which the pink and yellow streamers catch and the music is small, distant, wavering, as if the band were set adrift. His shirt is crisp and expensive and I sense he will never be without it, but I want to feel a little afraid. That's enough because the water is cool where I am living and yearn to live, on the inky, joyous lake-waves and the someone who holds me up there.

Another hot afternoon upstairs after school. I was half asleep. To cool themselves, small birds opened their beaks. They held their wings out for air, feeling dizzy in it. Small, white-hot birds, arguing about how small, how white, how hot they were. It was their way to begin making noise. They got used to it, grew stronger. The sound worked with the light into my nerves. I couldn't close my eyes because staring was part of the throbbing and the endless screen of trees full of silent, white flowers. The argument was inside, in places where I was thinnest. Back then, I could pull it to a hum and lie quiet till dinner.

Only talking. Only moving. On the terrace of the hotel, my mother ordered coffee. She read the paper, in front of Angel Island, in front of San Francisco. I was only doing one thing at a time. Watching her, watching the city, listening to her read about the deer. What we avoided—it's just noise, the way things go on.

Helen and I were cleaning the beachhouse. We were work-ing each other, starting to shout. I could hear both of us shouting at once and I could feel my heart as it spread itself throughout me and into what I saw of her—larger, smaller. Then there was nothing but Helen's laughter and sand blowing across the porch. As I stood waiting to leave, I was losing, finding out. In my unsteady hands, in listening to the whole sound. Bare nerve. I'd wanted to last with it.

Early, we heard new birds. In the weightless darkness, a velvet envelope, we lost sense of the words of fingers and lashes. The birds we called villagers, accidents, birds.

I liked curtains and eucalyptus. Lights in the rain. But skin and hair in their ceaseless adjustments became green hills, a warm ocean, complete, round horizon. I floated the way a heart floats in a body, the way life is buoyed by the blood without difficulty or rest; played with slight motion, once with the hand of a doll or toys I pulled near to me in fever, now the underside of your arm where the flesh is thin and hot, stems, watered silk, polished banister. It isn't all of love but beauty.

The marvel of glass and water. Siren, storm, footstep. Music and pictures. How all things change inside a person, settle and ride.

Above the Inland Empire today the sky is off the desert, deceptively active in a ridiculous heat. The whole country is hot, colored red-orange on the news. We are stuck here on earth with no breath of air. Coolers rumble all over town; I actually consider making lemonade. If there is a remedy, I will stay.

I was born into my skin and its future, the planet and its promise or demise. Each day a similar sun, the almost predictable moods of the moon, seasonal weather holding its shape for planned vacations.

After the earthquake this morning, the day broke sizzling with monstrous clouds to the east—what Mama once called "earthquake weather." I stood in the doorway until the windows quieted, and went back to bed, sleeping easily, rocking, anchored through dreams to the shifting plate. I trust the blatant forces, and worry only about that which grows and moves unseen, the odd cell, thriving.

Eileen, there is no way to practice traveling alone; you just go. And you might finally hear for yourself the stories you told us from your sleep. Maybe. Doesn't seem to matter how hard you try, you don't leave when you intended, and it's the idea of a cure, the reassurance of your own power, that defeats you. The world fails and you are a failure—not finding the impossible recovery that was set for you.

All disasters are natural. The heart shudders; the flood fills. No one knows what to die of.

We met as the names of cities and that made us laugh. In a drainage pipe in the Flintridge hills, Sydne and I were cold. We started playing with what we found: coarse gravel from the darkness, water, our bare arms.

We collected what our mothers threw out: greeting cards and broken lipsticks, and along with them we kept phrases as secrets. So in the twilight we saw mostly those things close or even in our hands. We heard our talking grow confused in the corrugated metal.

We got over our names. My fear and Sydne's thrill. The way anything came about was lost; we didn't need it. We wanted the chance that we had come with the stream of dark and heavy water, the runoff of a private storm that others would discover later. A fearless storm. Later. The day was ending outside us, around her flat-roofed house, out to her father's workshop, in the laugh she had—even for him. Before long, the differences in direction would be a matter only of touch and sound. A call from the house. The last glow on all that might keep us there and Sydne pulled me out through the tall, rough grass as if it were nothing to hear us leaving.

A storm of laughter. Provoker. I wanted the chance that everything and everyone belonged at least once, at least belonged to moving. The beginning would hold together without me; it couldn't explain our strong, short friendship or the dare I was taking from her there in the brush and dodder as she ran ahead, or the safety of the cold air and the smell of water that fell slowly over the metal lip to its mossy path. There was no way to figure through the darkness toward where Sydne must have been. Only what I knew of her that was only what she could do to me. The power of kind words and threats.

I always daydream good dreams, make imaginable only the best. I would say that we should leave this place, start over, knowing change is destined to be right. You would say, "Yes, we could do anything." I would tell you I admire you and you would believe me. The grand confrontations and cozy chatter are in my head constantly while I try to work or sleep or listen.

I try to think of anything else—complicated ideas, puzzles, or money. I would ask Jim to tell me if I make it difficult for him somehow and he would say I do. Though that kind of clearness is only fantasy, I pretend it strengthens me, that anyone could tell me anything and I would understand.

I don't know if imagining is fair. I don't know how it works into me, convincing me of friendship and success, but it's a chronic music to me now.

The sky would be cold over the city park, but I'd walk alone miles from there, out here, in Redlands, the "Friendly Place." And I'd wonder as I crossed to the fragrant groves if that long, low boom was the end of Los Angeles, about my sister, her new baby, and the uncountable bits of color and talk. Still, I would be telling them, they would be telling me. Still, someone's back is turned and the ugly worry leaks.

It's a real dream now, the patient one, the one that moans "Hold on" but offers no handle, no features. After straining in the haze, I carve out old photographs—of Kathleen and me in matching bathing suits in Balboa, of Chris the day his glasses were broken. Am I only juggling, like the cormorant fisherman, the lines between us, the tangle I mustn't doze from? "Attend," the birds whisper. "We quicken." But their wings don't move; their hearts don't beat; and the tiny earth attaches its body with invisible threads to the arguable melody.

Camellia, it's that moist and sensitive. It runs, instead, so pure through my veins, presses up at wrist and throat so delicate. World, tentative—pressing.

With licked fingers, I cleaned the cut on my ankle, pressed bougainvillea between a hollow sound of the canal at dusk and brilliant ideas. Love, meant to be remembered, rustles as pale liquid in parts of me that live outside at night with the killdeer that must be sleeping in secret in the cold.

Chilled, bare arms in the tunnel light. Breath whistles in the little cup. Stillness of these sheer petals—as cold and white as the moon, as the smeared streetlights of a tired drive.

Tonight is a face in the dark glass. The center, shop, restaurant are quiet. Something was not done. Goodbye. I feel the ghost of an underpass, black park, garage doors. Days don't begin each with the same potential. To believe they did was your protection, as was the morality which made a move a conscious choice. Good for that, but sad somehow.

The misery I hold is good sometimes too, for nights, coming into a cold room, sitting down with my coat on.